Based on real events

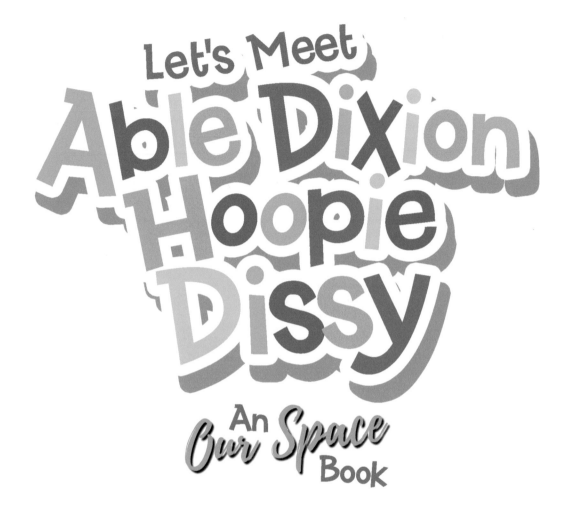

Let's Meet
Able Dixion
Hoopie
Dissy

An
Our Space
Book

Steven Botelho

Let's Meet Able Dixion Hoopie Dissy
An Our Space Book

iUniverse books may be ordered through booksellers or by contacting:

iUniverse
1663 Liberty Drive
Bloomington, IN 47403
www.iuniverse.com
1-800-Authors (1-800-288-4677)

ISBN: 978-1-5320-8221-4 (sc)
ISBN: 978-1-5320-8222-1 (e)

Library of Congress Control Number: 2019913497

Print information available on the last page.

iUniverse rev. date: 09/16/2019

This book is dedicated to all the children in
the world who question who they are.
What is it that you're meant to do? Tell your own story.........

Website: www.OurSpaceSafeSpace.com
Instagram: @OurSpaceSafeSpace
Facebook: www.facebook.com/OurSpaceTV
Youtube: OurSpaceSafeSpace

Special thanks to the Our Space family:

Tony Babcock: Editor, Assistant Director, and Show Host.

Stephanie Williams: Writer, Show Host, and Production Assistant.

Marlene Matos Jones: Show Host.

Diana Balogh-Tyszko: Show Host

Christian Bell-Young: Music composer.

Amanda Trapp: Music composer.

Hello Hello Hello!! My name is Able Dixion Hoopie Dissy, and I have ADHD. I am really special and I am just like you!

My mind has a lot it has to say, and a lot it wants to know. I can ask a lot of questions because I am curious about a lot of things and I am very smart!

Want to hear me play my Piano? Da da da da, doo doo doo doo, Dee dee dee dee. I just wrote it, it's called I want spaghetti for dinner.

I love to read books, reading is my favorite! I love reading books about Dragons, Unicorns, birds, adventures, Music, Christmas, and Halloween. I love Halloween! My costume this year is going to be a pine cone, last year I dressed up as a butterfly. Ooh, butterflies!!!

I love to swim in my pool, swimming is my favorite!
Marco, Polo, Marco, Polo! I'm hiding in
the bushes, I like this game.

I love to make up stories and tell them to my friends, these are my friends Lex, Auddy, and Anne. I have a great imagination! Once I had a dream I was a pirate sailing on clouds and a friendly monster made of cotton candy flew by me asking directions to the nearest candy cane land, and he was bright pink and blue and he had one big tooth. One day he.........

Ohh...I'm hungry!

But What happens next?

I love Vanilla Ice cream, Vanilla is my favorite! But I like to eat it in a bowl, I don't like to eat it in the cone,

I need a nap.

Sometimes it makes me upset when people think I am bad after being loud, or having a hard time staying still. My mom says it's because I interrupt people when they are talking. I don't do these things on purpose, but my mom is teaching me how to understand my actions. We talk a lot about it so that is how I am learning.

My ADHD is a part of me that I'm learning to control. I can be Impulsive which means I can make decisions without really thinking about the consequences. This is why I stand out. It's like I have my own superpower! You can call me Able Girl!

I am super special. I have friends and family that love me. I am unique. I am happy to be me, and I love myself! You want to know what else I love.......

Come closer and I'll tell you.........

I LOVE TO TICKLE!!!!

ADHD is a chronic condition marked by persistent inattention, hyperactivity, and sometimes impulsivity. ADHD begins in childhood and often lasts into adulthood. As many as 2 out of every 3 children with ADHD continue to have symptoms as adults.

Symptoms of ADHD can differ from person to person, but there are three basic types of ADHD. Each one is identified by the symptoms of hyperactivity, impulsivity, and inattention. When the main symptoms are inattention, distraction, and disorganization, the type is usually called primarily inattentive. The symptoms of hyperactivity and possibly impulsiveness appear to diminish with age but are seen in the primarily hyperactive/impulsive type. The third type has some symptoms from each of the other two and is called the combined type.

Please add this citation after definition:

WebMD Medical Reference Reviewed by Smitha Bhandari, MD on July 11, 2017

Sources

Printed in the United States
By Bookmasters